# Your Age
# Is Your
# Business

## HOW TO SELL YOUR WISDOM
## ONLINE & HAVE FUN DOING IT

To Railea, Lily, Leo, Kai,
Izzy, Max & Jed for reminding me
there is a new world out there.

# Acknowledgements

I would like to thank Taryn Johnston for rescuing this book from the toothless jaws of self-publishing. Sheila Murphy for meeting an impossible editing schedule. Joanna Urwin for sitting me on a pile of money. Gary Nightingale for his cartoons and Maya Saric who finally came up with a title that hopefully won't offend anyone. A special thank you also, to Ray Cooper, who encouraged me to write this book.

# Contents

# Preface

Last week I saw on the news that of all the people impacted by the unemployment situation surrounding Covid-19, the over-50s have been the hardest hit.

'Why?' I asked myself. Not 'Why are they unemployable' but 'Why would anyone with fifty years or more of life experience feel that they had to hang around, cap in hand, waiting for someone else to give them a job?'

As a 71-year-old I'm also curious about that joyful state they call 'retirement'. Surely the object of this whole exercise called living is to find a path that enables us to earn money spending all our time doing what we enjoy most – and who would ever want to retire from that situation?

The fact is that we have this wonderful (but sometimes scary) tool called the Internet and with that comes the opportunity to reach over 4.6 billion people, many of whom desperately need the benefit of our life experiences, our talents and our professional knowledge. And I promise you they are more than prepared to pay for it.

I've written this book because I would like to meet you and to show you exactly how you can sell your wisdom online and as you will find out, you can do that with minimal computer knowledge and even less money in the bank. If a complete technophobe like me can do this then anyone can.

Being broke or isolated when you are over 50 is no fun – choose not to be.

— Melinda Coss

# Disclaimer

This book is quite simply an 'un-training manual' applied correctly, the concepts here have the potential to make you extremely rich, devastatingly attractive, seriously uncompromising and extraordinarily happy. If as a result of these changes your partner leaves you, your children become concerned about how you are spending their inheritance and your friends feel uncomfortable with the new you, I hereby disclaim, on behalf of myself and my publishers, all responsibility. In writing this book I am assuming that you are a responsible adult with many years of experience under your belt and that you are more than capable of making your own decisions. Its sole purpose is to strip you of the limiting assumptions the world has taught you to make and to show you that life at any age can be a glorious, glittery journey of new inspiration and practical possibilities.

# Exclusions

Now I don't want to be picky here but when you have reached your diddly-something birthday, time really does become a nagging source of concern so I would hate it if I wasted any of yours. For this reason, I would suggest that if you cherish retirement for any of the following reasons (none of which I would presume to judge) it would probably be a good idea if you gave this book a miss:

» You just love your garden, reading novels, cooking, cleaning, watching television and knitting egg cosies. You are perfectly happy doing nothing else.

» You have a great pension and savings and the last thing you are interested in at your age is making more money.

» Being with your grandchildren is all you want from life and nothing gives you greater pleasure than dedicating all your time and energy to them ...give them a hug from me.

» You are perfectly content with your current circle
  of friends and enjoy your weekly get-togethers and
  the opportunity to hear and share with them news
  about all your various medical conditions.
» You are a technophobe and have no wish to have
  anything to do with computers, social media or
  any of the other new evils that have engulfed the
  younger generation.
» You love to receive all those stair lift ads that pop
  through your letterbox.
» You believe that living on a very tight budget is a
  lot of fun. Being prudent with your spending is a
  virtue, there are many in this world who are worse
  off than you and by not spending on or investing
  in yourself there will be more available for those
  with less... you're not quite sure how but you know
  you are doing the right thing.

I wish you well – but we are on a different wavelength.

# Inclusions

This book is for you if:

» You want to go back to work but you feel that no one will employ you now because you are too old.

» You've had a successful career that has finally got you to a comfortable retirement but you are secretly asking yourself what you are supposed to do for the next forty years.

» Your kids have grown up and left home, you are cooking so much that you've upped two dress sizes and you have completely exhausted everything worth watching on Netflix.

» You have a sneaky suspicion that your iPad was meant for more than chatting to your friends on Facebook and for playing solitaire. Everyone comes to you for advice on relationships/business/gardening/the stock market/cooking or some other unique skill you have and you are not charging for it. You are sick and tired of being broke.

# Translations

So now that I have you here I want to make sure you understand me: my editor tells me that I use some words my friends in the US may find too British/Yiddish. So here are the translations for you.

**Blimey** – OMG you're lying to me.

**Bloke** – Dude, everyday sort of down-to-earth guy.

**Boychick** – Mensch

**Broke** – Without Dosh (sometimes just a state of mind)

**Chutzpah** – Cheek, Nerve. Like, when at age six I wrote to Enid Blyton and told her she should give me a holiday job writing her books because I thought my stories were better than hers.

**Crikey** – OMG

**Dosh** – Money, Bucks, Dough, Moolah, Loot.

**Enid Blyton** – Best-selling English author of classic children's books like the Noddy and 'Famous Five' series.

**Fancy Schmancy** – Complicated and usually costs a
   lot.

**Kalooki** – Card game. A bit like Gin Rummy but with
   13 cards and lots of cheating.

**Latkes** – Jewish potato pancakes (if you haven't tried
   them you haven't lived!)

**Mensch** – Honourable young man (fit for a Jewish
   Princess).

**Meshuga** – Mad (but in a nice way).

**Popping your clogs** – kicking the bucket, dying.

**Programme** – English spelling of Program.

**Shidduch** – Match made in heaven.

**Woo-Woo** – People who believe that deep spiritual
   introspection, studying the Chakras or Tapping
   will earn them dosh (great when it works).

NB. If you see some other spelling that doesn't look right
to you (maybe extra 'u's or 's' used instead of 'z'), they
are not typos they are English spellings. Just don't want
you to think I'm illiterate here.

# Introduction

# So who am I to tell you anything?

This book is about you, not about me and I really don't want to bore you with my life history but I think I do need to explain why I feel qualified to write it so you can understand the context.

Right now, as I start writing I am wintering in a 5* hotel in Portugal. I am 71 and three-quarter years old and earn my living as and when I choose to as a life- and business-strategy coach. I wasn't born this way. I was, in essence, a child of the sixties, growing up full of belief that I could have anything I wanted (including a rich husband), coupled with emotional angst and general over-indulgence on shoulder pads, insecurity, lusts for sex and money and bucket-loads of guilt around the 'have nots'. Silly girl that I was, I then took to wearing flowers in my hair and walking away from all the material trappings in search of something more meaningful (think EST –running naked in a commune). In my early 20s, with no obvious career potential, I trod the prescribed middle-class boards of marriage (no, he wasn't the rich boychick I had been promised and I did marry secretly in my lunch hour, dressed head to foot in black), house purchase and children – followed just four years later by the essential nervous breakdown and divorce. Was it really my parents' fault? Was it hell! I am 100% responsible for the choices I made.

So, what do you do when you are divorced with three under-twos, no obvious education and no way to support yourself? You make a list of all the things you can do that could possibly earn you money. My list was very short: I could type, I wrote great letters and I could knit. I built three six-figure businesses on the back of those skills.

Post-divorce on my journey of self-discovery I raised three kids. (Well actually they raised me). I wrote thirty internationally published craft books.

I spent a year in LA working with movie stars and talent scouting for Penthouse magazine. I became famous at knitting. And ... I instigated and ran a big PR project for HM The Queen at Buckingham Palace.

After all that, somehow or other I created and headed up the largest handmade soap company in the UK.

More importantly those experiences gave me the tools that I will share with you here. And the reason I'm going to do this is because I know, categorically that it is never too late to start a business and that, no matter what your own life looks like, at no time in history has it been easier to find people who need and will pay for the lessons your experiences have taught you.

Being poor when
you are over 50
is beneath you.
Choose not to be.

# Chapter 1

# Discovering Your Wisdom

Despite all this frantic activity I had to wait until early on in my sixth decade before finding my true path to living successfully. The epiphany was simple. I suddenly realised that the things I had learnt in the wobbly, rewarding journey of my life were in fact my most valuable assets and that, with the help of this magical phenomenon called the Internet, I could share what I had learnt from my journey and could actually help lots of people, including myself, to live the life of their dreams.

I discovered to my huge amazement that, like fine wine, elements of my experience had magically matured into 'vintage, marketable expertise' and that by packaging up and selling that expertise I could earn myself more money than I ever did during the whole collection of successful and failed businesses.

...Who knew!

To recap, I had no formal qualifications, left school at 14 and have never worked for anyone other than myself for more than a month. If you've had an education, held down a job, had a successful marriage or lived through any life changing experience you have a much better chance than I ever did of monetizing your skills. You just need to learn how.

So, what will this new fancy-schmancy business of yours involve and what do you need to invest in it to make it work? Maybe I'm wrong but I'm going to assume that you do not want to spend your life stressed out or being glued to a computer. Nor are you driven to build yourself an empire. Isn't it true that most of us silver foxes/cougars just want to live comfortably, to feel secure and to be able to do what we want, when we want, surrounded by people who interest and stimulate us?

To help you understand what I want for you, here is a sketch of what my own life currently looks like:

I live in the southwest of France with my poodle, Doris, two pussycats and a couple of chickens. I work twelve hours a week mentoring my clients via Skype or Zoom (these are both free tools that you can download easily onto your computer). The mentoring consists of talking to and inspiring interesting people whom I have chosen to work with. I earn in excess of six figures per year doing just that. I also devote an additional eight hours a week working on (rather than in) my business exploring new ideas and producing useful content.

And the best thing is I truly help people. Every day I receive confirmation of that fact from clients whom I really love to work with. Do you have any idea what a gift that is and how good that feels?! Even if you don't need the dosh, working with people you love and who love you is a gift worth striving for. Many of my clients become close friends.

As I work entirely via Skype/Zoom and because I am on my own and now have the budget to do so, I choose to spend my life travelling to wherever I fancy working from. You might find me in Australia (hanging out with my son and his girls), in France where I have my home now, or in the UK (with my daughters and their kids). You might also discover me hanging out in the US or in Portugal, since all I need in order to generate income is a reliable Internet connection.

In short, I oversee my own life and can drop everything in order to spend great quality time with my three children and my seven grandchildren. And I also have enough money to help them when necessary.

I employ a part-time, UK-based, virtual admin assistant to take care of all the jobs I don't necessarily have to do or want to do myself. I get technical support from a lovely woman in Australia; my social media assistant lives in the Netherlands and my accountant lives on the other side of France. I have never actually met any of them but they all do a brilliant job. To support my business I pay for around 12 hours of freelance work per week, which includes my lovely cleaning lady and my gardener. This frees me up for the lifestyle I have chosen.

So what does your dream life look like? You really can have it, you know. Read on and we'll talk about how you can get to live a life that has you jumping or (in my case with my herniated disk) slowly climbing out of bed in the morning, looking forward to an interesting and stimulating day. I will also explain why this is the best time in your life to explore this journey and I'll help you avoid the traps that could stop you moving forward.

That said, although the concepts in this book, when implemented correctly, have the potential to make you a multi-millionaire, don't expect that to happen. Go into this simply because you want to earn some extra money and to challenge your ability to stay on top of this new and exciting digital world we live in. Take it slowly and take it step by step. You will learn how to build your income once you become more familiar with the tools you need to do that.

" Your dream business lies at the crossroads of:
Your expertise
Your passion
Your skillset and
Your network "

# Chapter 2

# Let's start by discovering your wisdom

To begin this journey the first thing we need to find out is what 'expertise' you already have that you can focus on and turn into dosh.

Expertise does not necessarily come from university degrees or work experience (although they can certainly help). When your hair starts to turn grey (and that's the sign of being truly grown up) 'expertise' can be measured by your life experiences, your personal achievements, your passion, and the problems you have managed to solve in your personal or professional life.

There are three main markets out there. The first is made up of people who want you to help them to earn money; the second is made up of people who want you to make them feel better about themselves, and the third is people who want you to teach them a new skill just for the fun of it. All these markets will invest money in your services if they are convinced you can solve their problem. The only difference is that if you offer a skill, which will earn people money rather than just make them feel better or entertain them, they will value this more highly so you can charge more for the advice.

The global eLearning market, which mainly involves online coaching and digital learning platforms, is expected to reach a combined value of more than $325 billion by 2025. This endlessly expanding industry provides extremely lucrative opportunities for those with the know-how to make the right moves.

— *Source:* www.entrepreneur.com

Let's put those facts into context: are you old enough to remember the sixties? What did your parents think when we were all screaming at the Beatles and wandering down Carnaby Street in London? Sixties music and fashion entrepreneurs made huge amounts of money because they tapped into a social need for freedom and change. The digital information revolution is exactly the same thing, except it is giving us what we want now and it has the ability to move ten times faster than we did then.

The most important concept I want you to grasp is the mind-boggling fact that while you are sitting there in your living room playing games on your computer or your phone, you have access to 4.6 billion Internet users worldwide. Just think about that, and while you're thinking ask yourself how many of them share an issue or life experience that you have lived through or overcome, or how many of them could benefit from the skills you have demonstrated during your working and personal life? The answer is that you need to reach just a tiny, weeny fraction of that number of people to provide yourself with a very nice income.

## All About You

Right now I want you to put down this book and make a list of all your accomplishments, both professional and personal. I want you to identify why people/friends/ former business associates might choose to come to you for help or advice and on what subject. If you have had a professional career, what did your colleagues consider to be your strengths and your weaknesses? What could you sail through that most of your peers had difficulties with? Maybe you were a great people-manager, could sell fridges to Eskimos, had strong organisational skills or were a whizz at cash flow planning and troubleshooting. Maybe your work put you in contact with a network of distributors, retailers or high flyers that other business- es would love to reach, or perhaps you were great at negotiation, managing in-house politics, handling large (or small budgets) or converting trucks into fast-food restaurants?

Perhaps you mastered one specific piece of complex software, or you know how to run a HR department – these are just a few of the skills you could package into an online teaching programme or consultancy service.

If you haven't had a profession as such then look at your life experiences. Maybe you had your children when you were very young, survived a divorce or perhaps you've picked yourself up after a specific illness that you could help people to deal with. Maybe you trained your

dog to cook the dinner, cared for an elderly relative or
found a way to deal with difficult teenagers or relation-
ship problems. Perhaps you are brilliant at interior
design, flower arranging, matchmaking or de-clutter-
ing, or maybe you speak another language fluently. It
might be that you're simply good at getting to the point
and helping people find their purpose. Whatever your
expertise you need to focus on something that you feel
confident you can help people with. I'm not talking
about a get-rich quick scheme here, we are looking to
find a genuine skill that you have but which, I suspect,
at this stage you don't recognise as a potential income
earner for you. The value of your skill will be evident
when you package it up into a programme (I'm going
to help you do that) put a price tag on it and learn how
to start selling it.

If you have a problem identifying your skill, just ask
your friends or family what would they look to you for
advice on? The subject really doesn't matter too much
because with 4.6 billion out there the chances are you
can find enough people who speak your language and
who are struggling with the same situation to ensure
you can build a solid and sustainable business. In fact,
and yes, I know it's counter-intuitive, the smaller your
niche the more chance you have of making individuals
feel special and of creating success for yourself.

I want to pause for a minute here with an aside to
my knitting, cake-making and craft-loving friends. While

I am sure (in fact I know) there is room out there for you to market your real-life products, this is not what this book is about. Having been in the product business for most of my working life I know that selling product involves investment, stock holding and bucket loads of your time, to make what will be a relatively small income. I simply don't think it's a rewarding journey to go on when you have better things to do with your energy.

However, if you can write up your processes and sell them either as an online programme or as a series of videos then there is a big market out there just waiting for you to do it.

Write that list and stick it on the wall so you can remind yourself just how brilliant you really are during those times when your confidence is waning.

# Chapter 3

# Meet Christine Camm

www.simplyfrenchonline.com/

*At 53 years young, Christine decided that she wasn't going to delay living her dream life any longer so she quit her lucrative teaching job in the UK and moved to France. She wasn't sure how she would replace her income but she just knew everything would work out fine.*

*Today Christine runs Simply French Online, offering one-to-one tutoring, group lessons and a very successful subscription membership to those who want to learn French. While it has taken her five years to achieve her success, she now feels solidly on track to earn €100k a year.*

*In order to gain the knowledge to do this Christine followed a number of online business influencers and took various courses such as Stu McLaren's TRIBE which taught her how to develop her membership. The hardest part of her journey was accepting that to succeed she needed to learn in her own way and at her own pace, and the best part has been discovering herself and what she is capable of.*

# If this is so easy why isn't everyone doing it?

That's a very fair question that I ask myself every day. Apart from the fact that many simply haven't thought about the possibility of selling their wisdom online, there are common stumbling blocks that stop people from even considering this as an option. Here are some of the ways your brain is likely to stop you in your tracks:

1.  *This is for other people but not for me*
Behind that statement lie years of conditioning designed to keep you in your place. If now is not the time to explore what you are capable of then when is?

2. *I don't know enough about my subject*
Known in the trade as 'imposter syndrome' this is a very common shortfall in confidence. Go back to the list of skills you wrote down earlier and ask yourself whether a 20- or 30-something really knows more than you do about your subject.

3. *I'm no good with computers*
I get that one because neither am I but luckily for us there are plenty of low-cost people out there you can pay to do the tech stuff for you. If you know enough to chat to your friends on social media, put together a Word document, send an email and upload a photo you have

enough computer knowledge to get something going. If you haven't yet mastered those skills find a course on basic computer knowhow. Once you overcome your resistance a whole new world will open for you.

Quick aside here. Have you actually tried to fathom your way through a computer problem or are you the type who throws their arms up in the air and hands the issue over to your tech star of a daughter, friend or grandson? I just ask this because sometimes we allow things to intimidate us when, with a little logical thought we could easily overcome and solve the issue ourselves ... and when we do manage to solve it, it is SO satisfying.

*4. I can't actually charge people for this stuff!*
Our attitude to money, what it is and what it's for is really weird, isn't it? While we know that we ourselves would see the value in paying for something that we believe could truly improve our lives in some way, when it comes to asking others to do the same we feel like we are committing a mortal sin. Some of this is tied up in imposter syndrome because the real truth is, unless you have a potential customer at gunpoint you are not going to persuade him or her to part with money for something they are not convinced they feel they want or need, because they think much the same way as you do about money. The people prepared to pay you for your services are those who are committed to learning from

you. The fact is that if they have to part with hard-earned cash in order to get what you are selling, they will value what you teach them. If they get it for free, they won't.

Another thing to consider here is that what other people spend their money on is actually none of your business. Your business is simply to present and supply the very best product/value/information you possibly can at a price that reflects that value. The hard truth is that if you don't believe in your value why should anyone else?

### 5. Inconsistency

I'm not going to lie here. If you want your business to succeed then in the early stages you are going to have to dedicate time, effort and commitment to it and your golden nugget is your ability to reach people online on a regular basis so that they can get to know and to trust you. Posting free information consistently is your key to success and to building a loyal following. Popping in just when you feel like it really won't serve you well.

### 6. Who wants to learn from an old person like me?

Oooh, this one makes me mad. You are not 'older', you have just been young for longer than younger people have and that fact alone means that you have vastly more life knowledge and professional experience than a younger person. Not only that but you have the advantage of being able to demonstrate that fact by allowing your wrinkles to twinkle (I stole that bit of cleverness). There is a difference between an old woman and a 'matriarch/doyenne' and an old man and an 'ambassador' and that difference lies solely in how you view and present yourself to the world. And if you are going to put yourself in the limelight please don't feel you have to get Botox or a toupee before you do so. (Really? Have you checked out my author pic – I'm practically bald!) Please believe me here, if your message is genuine and delivered with confidence people will love you and respect you far more if you go out there just as yourself, warts and all.

# Chapter 4

# How to find clients

As you get further along with this you will find that there are lots of ways to attract a cold audience of potential clients through social media but for now let's look at possibilities that can come through people you already know, i.e. your 'warm' audience. Because your warm audience is made up from people you can reach easily, this is the group you will feel the most comfortable talking to. It's also a great place to start to identify your ideal clients because you can talk to them (and write your programme) in a vocabulary that both you and they are familiar with.

If you are over 50 and trying to run a programme for 16-year olds you immediately have a barrier to entry because you simply cannot write and talk authentically in their language without being seen as patronising or completely ridiculous. If you don't believe me ask your grandchildren. Remember also that this should not be a heavy sell. What you are doing here is giving people the opportunity to buy a problem-solver or life enhancer that they really need. This is not the same as having a network marketing friend endlessly corner you in order to sell you a water filter, some ghastly chemically loaded shampoo or a load of Tupperware that you really don't want or need.

If you have (or belong to) any of the following then you already have a warm list: start by talking to them and telling them what you are proposing to do and see what feedback you get. Above all, always remember it's easier to build a product around a demand than it is to build demand around a product.

## Warm audience

» A group of personal friends and relatives
» An online or real-life interest group
» Past work colleagues
» Local community or religious group
» Facebook friends/groups
» Place of education (school, college etc., maybe through your kids).
» Social Clubs/Associations
» Or perhaps you still get on- or offline trade magazines or follow forums related to your previous line of work?

Here is a real-time example of how this works. This morning I posted on my Facebook page a copy of the disclaimer at the front of this book and asked my friends what they thought. In just one hour 25 people told me that they loved the idea and couldn't wait to buy the book. That means I have 25 potential buyers before I even complete it, and without doing too much work I have verified that I am on the right track. The chances are that those 25 people will tell their friends about the book or, if I ask them to, they will share the information on their Facebook pages. If their friends subsequently share the information with *their* friends, before you know it I've reached an audience in the thousands. So, what am I selling here? I'm selling a book that is outside the realms of my normal professional field. In fact, it's all about my personal experiences (vintage wisdom/expertise) around building a business whilst getting older. So I'm going in cold, just as you will be, and as you will see later on I have also created a programme to go along with the book and that programme will provide me with a revenue stream. So let's deal with how you create a product right now and then we will talk a little bit more about how you can reach a cold audience.

## Meet Jeff Walker

https://jeffwalker.com

*Jeff is a superhero multi-millionaire in the online course world but he didn't start out like that.*

*He started by offering stock market tips in a free email newsletter to a mailing list of 19 people. But he says:*

> *The problem was that I wasn't making any money. I knew I needed to sell something, but I kept delaying making that offer because I wasn't a sales-man – and I didn't know how to ask for the offer.*
>
> *So I kept delivering more value ... and when I finally made the offer, people were really excited to buy.*
>
> *I kept refining my 'launch' process, and the results kept getting better... until my formula was almost guaranteed.*
>
> *I started sharing what I learned about launching new products and businesses with some other entre-preneurs I knew. And their results were incredible. Pretty soon, I was getting asked to speak on stage and teach people about how they can use my formula to launch their own products and businesses. The amazing results continued to pour in – and that's when I decided to turn it into a step-by-step program that anyone could follow.*

*Jeff is the author of the* New York Times *bestselling book* Launch. *He has helped thousands of entrepreneurs at all levels to launch programmes that have in total generated over a billion dollars of revenue.*

*So you think you are no good at selling? Just consider: every time you persuade a kid to eat greens you are 'selling'. If you believe that what you are selling is right for your customer you can do it easily and with real conviction.*

# Creating your product

For our purposes a 'product' is informational content that can be delivered in any of the following ways:

» Emailed PDF document, files or newsletter

» Video media content (YouTube videos)

» Online or Skype one-to-one consultancy

» Online pre-recorded, self-learning programme

» Online instructed group programme

» Private subscription membership

» Webinars (online seminars)

» Podcasts (audio presentations)

Other than a computer, a phone with a camera and an Internet and social media account, you do not need specialist equipment to deliver any of the above formats although some basic extras could help. I will talk a little more about those later.

First you need to think about the content you would like to deliver and whether it is possible for you to break it down into topics as you would if you were writing the chapters of a book. So let's look at an example here. Just say that in a past life you were ace at selling (probably in a particular industry sector) and because of this you want to run an online group programme teaching others in that industry, how you managed to be top company salesman/woman three years in a row. Now make a list of between six and twelve critical actions or strategies that you believe would help someone make a sale.

Look at your programme from your potential client's point of view and decide what information they primarily need to get from where they are (struggling to make a buck) to where they need to be (salesperson of the year). The same would apply if you were writing a programme on 'How to crochet with your big toe' or 'How to climb from zero to hero in your corporate job'. Or maybe 'How you stopped your son playing truant', or even 'How to live with Tinnitus'. Perhaps you know loads about cactuses or you bake vegan cookies to die for? Write a list of the twelve most important pieces of advice you think your ideal client needs to know in order to master your topic because those pieces should be the foundation of your programme.

The most important factor in any online programme is that it takes people on a measurable journey from where they are to where they need to be.

The second thing you need to do is to decide exactly who you would like to teach this stuff to. Who needs this information enough to pay for it? Maybe it's for telephone salespeople (good choice Batman, there are millions of them out there). Maybe it is for estate agents, car salesmen, insurance salesman, corporate service providers, bored housewives: before you decide, ask yourself two questions:

1. Who would I most enjoy/feel comfortable working with?
2. Who considers selling to be a big problem and would therefore be willing to invest in this programme.

One of the most important factors in starting a business later in life is making sure that you are going to enjoy it. We certainly didn't get to this stage in order to take on a moneymaking but soul-draining burden. The social aspect of your business should be as enjoyable as the work itself, so teach what you feel confident and passionate about to people with whom you want to spend time.

## This is too easy, what's the snag?

I have been coaching would-be entrepreneurs for 15 years now and in my experience the biggest barrier to success is in your head. Why should it be otherwise? For generations we have trodden the familiar path of school, career, family and then that panacea called 'retirement'. And for many that is just fine.

If you have done well in life and can afford in your post-50s or 60s to sit back, eat the food, take in the sun and stay happy, then good luck to you. All that actually matters is your health and your security – but the fact is that at 60 our generation is actually 20 years younger than our parents' generation when it comes to health, fitness and brainpower, so why do some of us let the world treat us as if we are invisible or over the hill. It could well be that you still have 40 of your best years to come so why even consider hanging up your hat?

In my book (*ahh*, and that's where I am right now) if you have made a mint (or found the secret to contentment) you have actually reached the beginning of your journey, not the end. In this world and particularly in this time of viruses, floods, fires and God knows what other devastations, many of us want to give something back, something a little more valuable than teaching your grandchildren how to do The Twist or showing your daughter how to make latkes (although thinks... you could easily monetize that second option).

Another thing I'd also like you to consider is that your kids and grandkids may well be treading that same familiar path of school, job, family and retirement (mainly because you taught them to do so) but you would have to be pretty blind not to see that the world has changed beyond all recognition and because of technology it will continue to change 30 times faster than it did when we were growing up. Internet evils recognised and dispensed with, information is the largest and fastest growing currency in this big, messy, wonderful, multi-cultural world of ours and you don't want to go popping your clogs before you have reaped the amazing benefits, experiences and social interactions it can give you, now do you?

While on the surface, this book is about your ability to create money, it is much more importantly, about asking you to remember the huge contribution you have made in your life-journey. You need to know that you still have a great brain and the power to empower and inspire your future clients. You have the ability to help hundreds, even thousands of people earn their own money or simply to learn how to relax and enjoy a new skill.

This book will also show you how to build a network around you that will protect you from becoming that boring, lonely or needy old fart we all risk becoming. I want to encourage you to grasp and understand the amazing tools we now have at our fingertips and the far-reaching difference they can make to your life and the lives of your children and grandchildren. Your kids are living such different lives to the one you led and the challenges they will have to face are a million miles away from the ones you had to face. The problem is that if you are close to them and taught them well you need to recognise that a lot of what you taught didn't prepare them for the world they are living in now. We shouldn't dismiss things because we don't understand them; we should embrace everything that is new and temper it with our life experiences.

Your life/career/job may have been challenging, boring, exhausting or just a means to an end. Alternatively, it may have been stimulating and life enhancing. The point is that either way, the path you have earned yourself is the opportunity to create another life, one fundamentally based on passion, comfort, community and friendship. In this new career I want for you, 'you' determine those you work with. And once you have mastered how to do this and put in the time and effort necessary to do it you will put yourself 100% in control of how many hours you choose to work, what you choose to do and where you choose to work from.

Now I know that what follows is not true of all retirees so please forgive me if this isn't you, but I have found that retired people often suffer from some big issues such as:

» Loss of status: did you 'used to be' or are you still?
» Bad health traps: could you do more than you think you can? Quite possibly not, but a question worth asking yourself.
» Isolation: do you live for visits from the family?
» A need to save face: you simply can't afford to join your friends for that expensive meal?
» Loss of confidence: this new world is just too complicated?
» Boredom: knowing there is so much you can still do but thinking you will be considered too old to do it.

» Loss of self-worth: not believing anyone would pay for what you have to offer.
» Dependency: a big fear around becoming financially dependent on your kids.

If any of the above situations resonate with you then you need to put them in a box and mail them to someone else, but for now let's take a look at the flipside of those coins.

Imagine if you had:
» Increased status: you are the only person in your community who generates more money at 60 than they did at 30.
» Bad health traps: you have far more interesting things to think and talk about than your last operation. Maybe you could be the next Captain Tom?
» Isolation: you run a Facebook group with thousands of people on it who adore you (Hi Penny and Ronny).
» A need to save face: you'll go camping with the family but only if you can stay at the neighbouring Ritz Carlton.
» Loss of confidence: your grandkids come to *you* when they need their new phone set up.
» Boredom: your biggest concern is that time might be called before you have done everything you want to do.

» Loss of self-worth: people are queuing up to pay
  for your wisdom.
» Dependency: you are the one they come to when
  they need money. (OK, so you don't have to be
  home at the time).

# Chapter 5

# Meet Amy Scott-Maclean

www.wellnesswise.com

*Amy started her online business when she was 55. Her aim was to help people in midlife to lose weight. She delivers her cookery and exercise videos through a Facebook Group and also offers one-to-one coaching at an hourly rate. For additional revenue she seeks out sponsorship from food companies whose ingredients she uses in her recipes.*

*Initially her husband helped her with the tech side of her business and her son edits her videos for her. She promotes her services by being a guest Podcaster in other people's interest groups and by running promotions on Pinterest and in her Facebook Group.*

# Go away with your get-rich-quick schemes – I can't afford to do this!

... And who can blame you for thinking that. We are absolutely programmed to be risk averse and to protect ourselves from mad, elderly divorcees (particularly if we are an attractive widower still in charge of his faculties and his bank balance). But let me tell you a story.

Sixteen years ago, I sold up my UK business and home and moved to France. The old romantic, tumbledown farmhouse I bought did what all old romantic tumbledown houses do, it ate up all my money.

I should point out here that I am not by nature a saver. I have been through some brilliantly successful times and some very financially scary times so neither am I a worrier. In fact, my history tells me that I produce my best ideas and work when financially my back is against the wall. For that reason, if I'm operating on a full tank of dosh, I have great fun spending it. If the tank is empty, I have an equally good time coming up with new ways to fill it. Getting really rich doesn't interest me in the slightest but like all good Jewish girls I do like to maintain a fridge that will feed a family of eight for at least a month.

Anyway, there I was in France with two large poodles, a lovely young man I had collected along the way and a completely empty dosh tank. Apart from bits of consultancy work (for which I was grossly undercharging), I had no real plan and no direction forwards and the young man, bless him, wasn't in a position to keep me in my accustomed lifestyle with a taste for smoked salmon and my fast-accelerating old age.

Then I saw an online ad for a coaching programme. This business guru in the States was telling me that she could change my life and help me earn a fortune and she was asking me for 5 grand and adding that I would also need, at my own expense, to travel to Florida, Sydney, LA and Paris, put myself up in five-star hotels and attend her events. Go on, say it ... 'Meshuga' (I can hear you from here).

I had never been tempted by coaching programmes before, but I knew somewhere deep down that with all the life experiences and successes I had had in the past I shouldn't now be sitting in France with an empty dosh tank (if I was so clever then why wasn't I rich?), so something made me investigate further. Lo and behold, I found an old friend who, one year earlier had signed up for and completed the same programme.

Actually 'found' is an understatement. Suddenly every time I logged online my friend was there, looking beautiful, selling her own programmes and exuding success. I called her, got the rundown on the programme and within ten minutes flashed my credit card and found myself 5 grand poorer.

Looking around for someone to blame I decided the poodles had made me do it.

To add to my scepticism (and I should include here the scepticism from my kids when I told them what I'd done), during the first coaching call I became aware that this programme that had nearly bankrupted me was full of Woo-Woo. My coach prayed to the Universe, manifested things and wore nothing but Roberto Cavalli. Her ideal client was in fact around 20 years old, living in LA, spiritual and extremely aspirational whereas I, her latest recruit, was in my sixties wearing Ikea and about as spiritual as a cheese sandwich.

But the point was this. She was rich and I wasn't. She clearly knew something I didn't about this online coaching stuff and having invested 5k in her programme I was sure as hell going to make it work for me. Within one month of the six-month programme, following her advice to the letter I had got back double my investment and gained the courage to quadruple the consultancy fees I was charging and, on my morning walks of gratitude (have you seen *The Secret*), I managed to 'manifest' an endless stream of clients which five years later hasn't dried up. In fact, I have doubled the investment required to take my own coaching programme three times since then and the clients still pour in.

What should you take from this? It's really very simple: 'You think you can or you think you can't – either way you're probably right'. How you think and how you translate those thoughts into action are the keys to getting you anything you want in life – but you need the confidence to make a leap and invest in yourself, and the willingness to do the work to get you where you want to be.

NB. Read *Leveraging The Universe* by Mike Dooley.

Why is it that most of us accept without question the value of investing in our kids' university education but when it comes to investing money in ourselves, we let the guilt kick in?

I know what I am going to say next will be controversial so please don't pelt me with eggs. But I would really like you to think about the purpose of money in relation to your life now.

If you are anything like me, you were raised to value your security at all costs. Don't spend what you don't have, credit cards are evil, etc., etc. And if you were at a stage in your life where you had a family to support and were struggling to pay your rent/mortgage then I would totally endorse that view, but if you are post-50 it's very possible that you are now responsible for supporting only yourself.

If you are convinced that investing in yourself will give you a happier or more prosperous outcome, then why would you leave money in the bank where it's gaining very little interest – why not use it for an exciting adventure that will improve your life?

So, if you are telling me you cannot afford to invest in yourself how are you managing your money? Do any of these describe your money management plan?

» You have savings invested for a rainy day and you live frugally off your pension?

» You have a personal spending pot, a business spending pot and an emergency pot and you never dip into the wrong one?

» You have a small regular investment income that is generated by a largish investment that you will only touch in an emergency?

» You have a redundancy payment but you are loath to touch it?

» You have a big yacht in the harbour but have no intention of selling it no matter how many creditors tell you to.

The point is this: if you are not living your best life then any assets that don't improve that situation are not worth hanging on to; life is too short and unpredictable. However, before you liquidate them or dip into the wrong pot you need to feel confident that your idea will give you the return on investment that you need, whether that is money, confidence or a more satisfying lifestyle.

Investing money in coaching programmes or business ideas just doesn't work unless you are committed to seeing them through to profit but if you feel you can do that then do it now because you might not be in a position to do it later.

Your purpose is to live the very best life you can and if investing in yourself will make that happen for you then don't let the fear gremlins stop you.

## Mechanics

Whilst I firmly believe that your 'Why' (personal motivation for doing this) is more important than your 'How' (the mechanics that are going to help you do it). I am going to teach you how to create a market and sell your information online and in order to do that you need to grasp a few bits of online marketing knowledge. To help you understand this I have composed the following list of online terminology that, if you are not familiar with it, might possibly confuse you:

# Acronym and Jargon Definitions

**Affiliate Partner:** An established entrepreneur or company with a large mailing list who is prepared to promote your programme for a commission.

**Apps:** Applications. All kinds of relatively low-cost or even free bits of software that will enable you to do clever things like adding subtitles to your videos or making sure your lipstick is the right colour. Some apps are free, others can be bought outright and some require you to take out an annual subscription.

**Blog:** Online living room where you can journal, share news and information, entertain your following and recommend products from which you will earn a commission.

**Facebook:** An amazing place where you catch up with old friends, make new ones and sometimes sell them stuff. Best if you want to attract the over-30s.

**Host (or website platform):** The company that sells you the technology behind your website and also rents you the real estate where you park it.

**Instagram:** Same as Facebook but you do it with pictures. For business it's best used if you want to sell to under-35s. (NB. As Facebook now owns Instagram you can post in both places at once).

**Landing Page:** This is a URL (see below) you send people to when you want them to get the message and take action quickly without having to wade through your whole website in order to find your programme offer. Landing pages can be used for signing people up to Webinars, giving them access to free goodies or providing them with a taster of your programme. You can buy products that make it easy for you to create loads of landing pages or you can just create an extra page on your website as every page has its own unique URL.

**Learning platform:** Password-protected, exclusive, online clubroom and place where you can store information and entertain your clients. Some learning platforms also host your website and mailing list and send marketing emails out for you.

**LinkedIn:** Great place for business-to-business marketing and for rekindling former professional relationships and making new ones. Also a good place to find experts and influencers in your field.

**Opt-In Box/Page:** An annoying pop-up box on your website that persuasively invites people to give you their email address so that you can add them to your mailing list and regularly tell them what you are up to.

**PDF (Portable Document Format):** A document created as a .pdf cannot be changed by the recipient. I'm sure there are other advantages to this format but I have yet to find them.

**Pinterest:** Brilliant visual treasure trove and idea resource, also becoming an interesting platform for selling.

**Podcast:** Your very own radio show – similar to Webinar but no video required.

**PowerPoint:** A piece of software by Microsoft that allows you to create slide-show presentations. There are plenty of other apps out there that will also allow you to do this (Google 'Best App for creating slide show presentation') but PowerPoint is the original so I've kind of stuck to it.

**Product:** The information you are going to sell.

**Programme/Program:** The package you are going to put your product in to make it easy for people to buy.

**Sales Page:** C'mon, I'm not going to insult your intelligence but if I must, the clue is in the name.

**TikTok:** The noise your clock makes.

**URL (Uniform Resource Locator):** Why on earth don't they just say 'Website address' because that is what it is? To help out your memory use this cue: 'Uncle Reuben's Lobotomy'.

VA: Virtual Assistant or, in the case of my team, 'Virtuous Assistants'. Online freelancers who take care of all the heavy lifting for you. Think: secretaries, technical geniuses, social media managers, researchers, coaches whom you pay by the hour and will probably never meet in person.

Webinar: A place where spiders demonstrate their creative brilliance and superior knowledge with the sole purpose of showing off and pulling in a captive audience.

Website: Your online holiday home and income creator.

Zoom: An online meeting platform where you can run and record live workshops.

# Chapter 6

# So What Will Getting This Business Up And Running Cost Me?

Good question! It kind of depends how fast you want to see a return. As I mentioned earlier, you probably already have the basic stuff, i.e. phone with camera, Internet and social media accounts and you can get a long way using free marketing techniques. But, they do have a steep learning curve and, in my experience, if there are things to learn or do that are outside your comfort zone, it's much cheaper in the long run to invest in freelancers who know what they're doing and can save you putting your fist through your computer screen or worse still throwing the damn thing out the window.

There are loads of online freelance agencies out there where highly professional people from all over the world are moonlighting to earn extra cash.

Check out the following:
» www.upwork.com
» www.peopleperhour.com
» www.fiverr.com

All you have to do is put in the job you want completed and then freelancers will come back to you with quotes.

Check out their references, and if this is for something on-going it's a good idea to discuss it with them via Skype or Zoom so that you can make a human connection and it doesn't feel like you are working with a robot from another planet.

Once you get confident at judging people you could look at some of the agencies in the Philippines where you can find incredibly cheap and efficient Virtual Assistants.

The first thing to know on this journey is that Google is your best friend. It can find anything you need to find, just be sure to make your search queries very clear: 'Virtual assistant with experience in programme launches' should find you what you are looking for in a general VA or if you want help with a particular App or Website platform you need to specify that is what you are looking for.

Likewise, if you find yourself with a technical problem, before you ask someone for help check out YouTube. com – someone is certain to have made a video that will solve the issue for you and make you feel incredibly clever because you sorted it.

There are also online agencies and associations for VAs in the US and the UK and, on average, you can expect to pay between £20–£35 an hour, depending on their technical skills. I retain a UK-based VA for 10 hours a month to act as my secretary and front of house person. She is my first stop for new client enquiries, sends out my marketing emails, organises my calendar and helps me manage my Facebook groups and product launches. Then I use a technical VA in Australia whom I pay by the hour as and when I need her to manage my website and learning platform (more about those soon) and to deal with clients who need help accessing info – usually because they have forgotten their password or haven't bothered to read the email you sent them.

Having Virtual Assistants in different time zones is also helpful as I can give them a task before I go to bed and it's all done by the time I wake up.

In short, if you want to keep your costs really low you can of course do everything yourself but in my experience that is a totally false economy. Getting help will dramatically speed up the process and spare you having to spend hours doing stuff you are not really interested in doing. Decide whether you just want to dip your toe in the water or if you really want success to happen for you.

While you can start out your project with just a simple Facebook page and Facebook Group, eventually you will also need a website. If you want to set yourself a challenge and think you might enjoy designing one play about on https://Wix.com (even I can use that). It's free to start with; the fees kick in only when you begin offering products for sale on there. Or check out https://Squarespace.com.

Of the two, IMHO, Wix is the most intuitive and easy to use but it doesn't have all the bells and whistles that a WordPress (www.Wordpress.org) website will give you. If you talk to a techy person who knows about this stuff they will inevitably recommend WordPress but I personally find those sites a nightmare to work on. They just don't think the same way I do and they need continual updating. Of course, once again, if tech is not your thing just Google 'cheap website packages'. There are loads out there on offer and for less than £500 you should be able to get a website designed and set up for you with everything you are going to need to begin with. One word of warning on these: before going ahead be sure to work out what making changes to your website will cost because these companies often make their money by offering 'maintenance packages' that can cost you an arm and a leg. Also make sure that you own the website and can transfer it, should you wish to do so at any time. It might be better for you to find a freelancer through one of the agencies I have given you above and pay them to create and maintain your site for you.

You will also need to buy a website address (URL) for your business and, since you are going to want an international audience, try and get a .com extension rather than .co.uk or anything else that suggests to viewers that you are only serving your country of origin.

If you use the website providers I have suggested, i.e. Wix or Squarespace, you can buy your URL through them. Alternatively check out www.namecheap.com. If you are not in the US avoid GoDaddy; it's complicated to get a security certificate from them and, without one, when people log on to your site they may get a message telling them they are in a 'danger zone' and should run away immediately. To clarify: if a site address begins with 'https' it is a secure site. If it begins with 'http' it isn't.

You want your URL to be easy to find so, if possible, use a simple name that clearly describes what you do. 'Freda's Floral Fantasies' might sound very pretty but 'Freda's Floral Design Courses' will get you faster to the people who need to find you. That said, if you already have a reputation in your field then by all means just use your name with a subheading on your webpage that states clearly what you do. That way search engines like Google will be able to find you easily.

Fashions in website graphics change regularly and at the moment a single scroll-down page that stretches to the edges of your screen is very much in vogue. All the website platforms I have suggested above offer various design templates but you don't want an old fuddy-duddy look with a central panel and menu tabs – go for something that looks contemporary.

# What do I put on my website?

I go into this in depth in my programme because, if you want to attract clients there is a science to the way you structure your content but for now, know that your website will need to contain the following information:

» A clear irresistible statement describing what problem you solve or learning delight you offer.

» The reason you are offering it, i.e. your story or something that expresses your credibility or experience.

» A 'Work With Me' section describing your product offers.

» A Shopping Cart set up so people can click on your products and instantly buy them or enrol in your programme.

» Your contact information.

You will also need what is called an 'Opt-In' box. That is one of those annoying pop ups where people are invited to fill in their email addresses and give you permission to mail them, usually in return for an incentive of some kind (maybe a discount on your services or a PDF with some useful information in it). The person who creates your website can also link your Opt-In box to a service/ website that will store and manage your clients' email addresses, see: www.mailchimp.com (start off with their free package) This is really important as email marketing still offers one of the most effective returns on investment in terms of product promotion: you really want to build a list of potential clients so that you can mail them on any news you have or announcements about the new programmes you are going to launch.

# Meet Cheryl O

www.cherylo.ca

*Cheryl is an artist living in Canada and at 66 years old she decided to run group painting and drawing courses online using Mighty Networks as a teaching platform and a place where her students could share and get feedback on their work. www.mightynetworks.com*

*She made this decision just as Covid-19 was about to hit and is delighted with the response she is getting.*

*Next year Cheryl also plans to expand her business by launching a private membership site and she has set her income target at Canadian $50,000 for the year.*

*Keeping your followers loyal by staying in contact with them is a critical factor for your success. It is eight times easier to sell an additional product to an existing customer than it is to attract a new customer.*

*Facebook Groups and Instagram are great tools for building an audience and getting followers but the only names/contact addresses you actually own are those on your own mailing list. Fortunately or unfortunately (depending whether you are buying or selling) a data protection act exists that forbids you to email strangers without their permission. You need to include a statement on your website to show you are complying with this. Once again, I will cover this in more depth in my programme and provide you with templates you can use. Or, if you are in the EU and the kind of person who wants to get all the information under their belt then here is a link where you will find it: www.gdpr.eu/ privacy-notice*

# Meet: Gary Nightingale

www.garynightingalebusinessillustration.com

*Gary made a living for many years as a highly paid sales- man in the computer industry.*

*In his early 50s he found himself floored by a messy divorce and decided that if he was going to start over he wanted his life to be on his own terms, away from the stresses and strains of corporate life.*

*Although not a graphic designer, Gary loved doodling and discovered that people around him appreciated his car- icatures and his humour so he set up as an illustrator and promoted himself through LinkedIn to corporate clients who wanted fun illustrations for their sales presentations.*

*Two years on, Gary is now making a fulltime living doing what he loves to do most. If you want to see his work check out the landing page for my programme at https:// www.melindacoss.com/wisdom*

# Chapter 7

# Curveball for introverts.

I am more than aware from my work with entrepreneurs that many people cringe at the thought of being 'visible' online. I think they feel that when they go on video people expect them to look like they have just escaped from a Chanel boutique, completed a course as a toastmaster and are word- and picture-perfect. Nothing is further from the truth. Today, more than ever, visibility and video marketing through Webinars (online seminars) or Instagram stories is hugely powerful but authenticity sells far better than polished performance.

I remember when I did my very first Webinar, I was in my son's basement in Australia and it was 2a.m. I truly was not dressed, made up or prepared in any way for the occasion but I talked for half an hour, from my heart, and while doing so the Internet connection went down three times. The result of that Webinar was eight new one-to-one consulting clients (think 24k) who all signed up within 24 hours. OK, so maybe talking is my secret weapon.

# What is a Webinar?

A Webinar is an online seminar/presentation during which you charm and delight a group of people that you have invited to join.

Webinars can be used to promote a programme or can make up part of your actual product.

When used for promotion Webinars are offered for free. During the Webinar you give your attendees loads of information and generally help them to get to know, trust and love you. Zoom is a great tool to use for this. (You will only need their 'meeting room' option, not their 'Webinar' option). The format you choose depends on what you are most comfortable with. Some presenters use PowerPoint or a similar App to create a slide show that they share with their viewers and talk through, some Webinars are presented in an interview format or you can just talk to your audience with absolutely no bells or whistles.

At a critical point during the Webinar, you tell your viewers about your product and give them the opportunity to buy it from you there and then, usually giving them an incentive (maybe a discount or a bonus) if they act quickly.

The most powerful Webinars are live broadcasts that include some time for questions and answers from the viewers, but if you're terrified at the thought of going live you can of course pre-record your presentation on

Zoom and simply invite people to come and see it on a specified date and time. Or you could post your recording on Facebook.

If I am doing a Webinar to promote a new programme I actually use an App called EverWebinar (www.everwebinar.com), which enables me to upload my recording but appears to everyone watching as if I am running it live. When people register to watch it they are given specific times and dates to log on although in reality the Webinar is running every 15 minutes around the clock for as long as I ask it to. Such clever stuff.

Once again, at the risk of being pushy, I want to stress that there is a science to how you structure your Webinar content to attract the most sales and I will cover this in depth in the programme I have put together to support this book (www.melindacoss.com/wisdom)

# Better done than perfect.

If you are really too shy to front your business in person, ask yourself what you are scared of. You're going to talk with passion about something you absolutely know and understand. You are offering to help people to make their lives more prosperous, interesting or to solve a difficult problem for them. Maybe you're going to demonstrate what fun it is to paint with watercolours (using just your nose) or how easy it is to make the best apple strudel in the whole world. Bottom line is people will either like you (the likeability factor is really important) or they won't, and often that choice says more about them than it does about you. If they don't sign up you've lost nothing, but they have lost an opportunity. This has cost you nothing except time. In reality, people don't stop to judge you or ridicule you; they are much too busy worrying about what others think about them! Just move on, try it differently or try something else.

Have I convinced you to come out of hiding yet? If not, you could of course offer the same material as a podcast, i.e. you talk through a presentation with no video – or you could even create a cartoon character and use it in your Webinar to represent you. But people like to buy from real people, and having an audience get to know, like and respect you is a very important key to your success and also to your own self confidence, going forward. Try videoing yourself on your phone, it's a great way to find out if you are constantly scratching your ear, using a nervous giggle as punctuation, filling the gaps with 'Uhh', 'Mmmm', 'OK', 'know what I mean' or 'I don't mean to be funny but ...' and you can avoid those traps next time.

# Learning platforms (used for group programmes).

When I started out I delivered all my programmes easily and simply on a free Facebook Group and that is how I would advise any beginner to start. Facebook Groups are great because they provide a place where you can build a community of peers with shared interests and community is powerful because it takes a lot of the heavy lifting and engaging off your shoulders. Your audience will talk to and inspire each other and not look to you to provide all the content yourself. You can create Rooms in a Facebook Group and do live or uploaded video training or you could kill two birds with one stone and put your videos on a free YouTube channel and then just share the link to them in your Facebook Group.

Another advantage in using Facebook is that it is likely your audience is already hanging out there. This means that when you post something new they will immediately get a notification and will pop into your group to see it. If they have to leave Facebook, get dressed up and go to your learning platform then it's more of a hassle for them.

If you are tech-shy I would recommend that you stop reading and set yourself up a Facebook Group right this minute so you can see how easy it is. The only frustrating thing about Facebook is that it changes the rules/layout/features all the time, so if I gave you step-by-step info on how to do this now, it might be out of date by the time this book is published. Instead, go and check out Facebook's own instructions—just type ,"how to set up a group" when you are in Facebook itself.

The one thing I would say is that when you get to the privacy settings, keep it as 'public' for now because once you set it to 'private' Facebook won't allow you to change it to 'public' and initially your aim is to get as many people in there as possible. In my programme I will talk about groups in depth as there are many tricks that will help you to build an audience but for now let's just get your group up and running.

You can also do live trainings on Zoom (once again, free to start with) and Zoom has the advantage of allowing you to have all the participants of your programme visible on your screen and they can ask you real spoken rather than typed questions. Zoom works really well for group programmes. If you want to get super clever you can 'share' your Zoom sessions by streaming them into your Facebook group so that people in different time zones can watch the recording as and when it suits them.

The only problem with working via Facebook is that, as I said earlier, you do not own the platform and Facebook algorithms change regularly. If you want to offer 'lifetime access' as a selling point for your programme you will need your own learning platform.

Learning platforms come in all shapes, sizes and price points. I now use Kajabi, which is an all-singing, all-dancing platform that also hosts my website and my mailing list and offers me the facility to involve myself (or I should say my VA) in complex data analysis and email list segmentation. So, for example I can specify exactly who I want to send an email to, based on all sorts of different criteria: maybe I want to mail people who opened my first email but didn't respond or who watched a Webinar and looked at my webpage but didn't sign up to my programme. As I said, if you want to take this seriously and reach thousands of people (which I do but you may not) you or your VA needs to get to grips with the science.

At the time of writing Kajabi costs me £159 a month, but unless you are a geek you honestly don't need anything that powerful to start off with – it's too much of a learning curve and you want to be sure that your product is going to give you a return on investment before you buy anything as serious as Kajabi. Other simpler and much cheaper learning platforms worth looking at are:

www.teachable.com

www.groupcoachinggenie.com

www.learndash.com

The final tool you will need is a service that offers a facility for you to take payments. I use www.stripe.com and you can also look at PayPal (www.paypal.com) although the latter is slightly more expensive in terms of the commission they take. When you use these payment platforms people can pay you in any currency just using their credit or debit card. Some website platforms dictate which service you should use but I think most of them allow you to use both or either of those two.

So, in terms of 'what will this cost', so far we are looking at getting you to invest in an up and running website and maybe some freelance help. In addition to a few hours a month of admin and tech help, you may need someone to create some graphics for you so that you become a brand. It's important that when people stumble on your social media posts they will know from the logo, colours and fonts used that this is you and not a cheap imitation. There are plenty of graphic designers to be found in the freelance agency links I gave you above, or you may have a friend or family member who would love to do this job for you.

Going forward, you might also want to invest in some Facebook or Google advertising; these work on a 'pay per click' system and ask you to set the budget for what you are willing to spend. In order to do this you will also have to set up a Facebook Business Page, as you can't place ads using your personal page. Facebook ads can produce great results because you can tell Facebook exactly who you want to target, where they live and what they had for dinner (not really but almost). But a word of warning here: get a freelancer who knows what they are doing to set these up for you – don't try and muddle through on your own or you could waste a lot of money.

The other investment it's important to consider is the time and energy it will take you to make this happen – but that, my friend, is true of every aspect of your life. You already know that what you get out of things depends entirely on what you are prepared to put into them, right? I repeat, this is not a get rich quick scheme. Like any business in the early stages, it requires work and some money. What it doesn't require is rent, rates, shop leases, stock, staff or any of the other risky financial, long-term commitments that building a business used to require. If your programme doesn't work for you, scrap it and try another topic. I have been known to get new programmes up and ready to launch in less than two weeks and at no additional expense except my time.

And if you spent your life working for other people remember you no longer have a boss and are answerable only to yourself. How good does that sound?

Crikey! Did that website and learning platform stuff feel like too much information?

I can see how it might have but honestly, don't worry about it. The mechanics of getting your programme up and running will become easy when you are clear about what it consists of and are motivated to get it out there. The best way to eat what feels like an elephant is one bite at a time so, right now, go for a walk, prep supper or do what I am about to do and go take a snooze. When we come back I'll talk to you about various ways you can offer your services so that they are stress-free and enjoyable to deliver. See you soon.

Break for Melinda's snooze

Zzzzzzzzzzzzzzzzzzzzzzzz.

# Chapter 8

So I'm back and feeling bright eyed and bushy tailed and I hope you feel refreshed too. Now, before we move into how you are going to actually package up your programme, let's recap for a moment and see how far you have come:

By now I'm hoping that:

» You have decided where your wisdom lies and what topic you are going to help people with.

» You know who your ideal client is and you have begun to think about where to find your initial clients.

» You have decided to create your own website or you have found a company that could do it for you.

» You have had a think about what areas of your business set-up you should farm out to a freelancer and what areas you are comfortable taking on yourself.

» You have explored the learning platform links I have given you and have also taken a look at Facebook Groups and you have decided on what you will use to begin with.

» You have set up your very own Facebook Group.

If you haven't done any of the above, do them all before you move on.

And to those who have, Wow! Well done.

While we are recapping let's have a think again about why you are doing this? Perhaps, like me, you still want to build an empire or maybe you just want to promote your passion and run something as a side gig. Could be you like the idea of building a community around you and are charging a little bit for this to make it interesting or perhaps you just want to stretch yourself and see what you are capable of. Whatever your motivation, set yourself a target for the additional income you want to earn from this over the next twelve months and then write down exactly what you are going to spend it on. Now stick that on your fridge and leave it there until you have achieved your goal.

If your motivation is more social than financial (and that is an excellent reason for taking this journey), how many people do you want in your tribe and what activities will you plan for them? I have online cocktail parties with my Facebook Group and we also meet up in person once a year for tea at the Ritz. Because of this personal connection they stay loyal to me and I love them to bits.

# Meet Jackie Bailey

https://speakfeedlead.org/

*Jackie started her career as a dental management consultant and then went on to do a course and become a toastmaster.*

*She realised quite soon the value of confidence gained when you can communicate well verbally and she started a business teaching children those skills. This business funded a social enterprise providing verbal communication skills to children whose families could otherwise not afford it.*

*Because of online access she can now deliver that programme worldwide.*

*Jackie promotes her business by using Affiliate partners who have larger mailing lists than hers. (More about that later).*

Now back to mechanics.

# How to deliver your wisdom

Up until now, the tools I have suggested are needed if you are intending to run a live group programme. What I like to do when I come up with a new idea is to run a live group programme in the first instance and record it.

Zoom allows you to record at the click of a button or, if you use Facebook Live, you can present your training by downloading a recording directly from your Facebook page or group.

My programmes usually consist of six or twelve, half-hour or one-hour Webinars (depending on what the topic requires), each with 15 minutes allowed for Q&As at the end. I also include downloadable worksheets for attendees to fill in. As part of the package I set up an exclusive Facebook Group where programme participants can keep each other accountable or where instructional videos can be shared. Sometimes I might also offer some pre-recorded interviews with experts on specific topics. I would run a programme like that over 12 weeks and deliver the Webinars either once a week or once every two weeks. Offer what you feel most comfortable with.

Once I have completed the programme and have hopefully got some endorsements from the participants, I get my techy lady to edit out the Q&A sessions at the end of each video and then I sell the package of recordings and worksheets directly off my website as a 'self-learning' package that customers simply click, download and buy. I usually sell these 'click and buy' programmes at half the price of the original live programme. This creates passive income for me and I can tell you there is nothing sweeter than waking up in the morning to discover that twenty people bought and downloaded my programme during the night and all I have to do for that is bank the money.

It is also a good idea to have somewhere to store your videos/Webinar recordings so that they are not taking up space on your computer. For this you can use www.vimeo.com or https://youtube.com. Both these platforms give you the option to keep your videos private and available only to people who are given a link. This is the option you should choose if the videos make up part of a programme you are selling. You can also use Vimeo and YouTube as revenue-earning channels in their own right.

The beauty of group programmes is that there is no limit to the amount of sales you can achieve and also, if you love working directly with people, they give you the opportunity to offer each individual in the programme at least some one-to-one, tailor-made advice depending on what they need. In terms of work, once you have the bones of your programme sketched out and you are pretty sure what you want to talk about in each session, you don't have to create all the content up front. You are going to spend around 50 minutes a week (or a fortnight) delivering your presentation, you need to pop on to your Facebook Group a couple of times a day to see if anyone has any questions for you and you may need to put together some worksheets. Job done.

The amount you charge for a live programme depends very much on your area of expertise and your credibility but for me (and remember I am teaching people how to make money) I would normally price a live programme at around £950–£1500 and would expect to sign up at least 25 participants. I also offer participants an installment plan where they can pay monthly but I charge an additional 10% for this to cover the admin.

## Affiliate Partners

Sometimes, if my programme is going to be aimed at a cold audience, I will find other groups or entrepreneurs with much larger mailing lists than I have to act as 'Affiliate Partners' by promoting my programme to their audiences. The commission they would receive for making sales would be anywhere between 10% and 50% of the price of the programme, depending on the size of their following. If you feel you can comfortably serve a large audience then the commission you have to pay really doesn't matter, as you will also have the benefit of loads of new email addresses you can market to when you launch your next programme.

Interestingly, I recently launched a programme where I offered Gold or Silver plans. The Gold plan included a Facebook Group and six one-hour group Q&As with me. The Silver plan, at half the price, was entirely self-learning and participants had no direct access to me at all. The Gold plan outsold the silver plan three to one so, more than ever now, people value and will pay for personal contact.

There are of course many other ways you can choose to deliver your knowledge and the method you choose should depend on:

» What you feel most comfortable with.
» What your clients will most benefit from.
» How much time you are willing to invest.

# Chapter 9

# What are the options?

## One-to-One Consultancy

This is your top-level option and the one that you can charge the most money for. You can approach this in several different ways according to the time you feel it will take to deliver the results you want for your clients or the time commitment you yourself are willing to spend in your business.

A one-to-one consultancy package could consist of:
» A single one- or two-hour consultation that will solve a particular problem for your client.
» A package of, say, six hours of consultation so you can be on call to help your client complete a project.
» An annual retainer that gives your client xx hours of your time a month.

There is a real advantage to presenting your package options clearly on your website because it makes the process of buying your services much easier for your clients. If you are vague about the choices, they often end up not making any!

The hourly rate you charge depends on your field of expertise so look around and see what other consultants in your business are charging for their services. Once again, if you are helping people to earn money you can charge more than if you are teaching them a new hobby or making them feel better.

Actually, there is an exception to this rule. If you build your reputation as an expert in making people feel better, you can charge a great deal of money. But you really have to put yourself out there and get known before you can do that. I believe my former coach now charges her clients around US$30k to spend the day with her, while my current coach charges US$75k a day and I'm really not brave enough to ask him what he offers for that, but I suspect it's interesting.

Normally the more hours a client commits to, the lower the hourly rate. Payment terms, except for the retainer option, should be 100% up front. Or you could offer two- or three-monthly instalments with a 10% reduction if the client pays up front in full. NB. Be careful here not to suggest an all-in price first, with a supplemental charge if they pay by instalments, as it is illegal for you to be charging 'interest'.

A one-to-one consultation can be delivered on Skype or Zoom or even on WhatsApp or (if Covid-19 is out of the picture by the time you read this book) then in person.

## Self-Learning or Click & Buy Programme

A self-learning programme can consist of any combination of video presentations, Webinar recordings, workbooks or PDF informational handouts. You package them together, advertise the package and your customers can just click, buy and download. Voila! The downside is this option requires you to have everything done and dusted before you start selling. There are also many free click and buy programmes out there so, unless you have stumbled on a really desirable and exclusive niche topic you are limited in what you can charge. Self-learning programmes typically require a high level of promotion for you to sell them. The upside is that you earn money while you sleep, i.e. you have a product that can earn you passive income ad infinitum.

Make no mistake, if you get the marketing of self-learning programmes right you can make a lot of money. One close associate of mine (who, I want to point out, is a hugely dedicated and knowledgeable online entrepreneur who invested several years building her audience) markets a suite of very niche self-learning programmes twice a year and makes over a million pounds out of every launch.

Remember there are 4.6 billion potential customers out there. Being 'Niche' and becoming the go-to expert in a limited arena can be hugely powerful and financially rewarding.

Oh, my goodness, look at the time! I get so excited when I'm talking about this stuff that I completely forget my poor poodle Doris, who is right now standing by the door with her legs crossed. It's a beautiful day here in France and I'm going to go out and get some fresh air.

See you later. When I come back I will tell you all about the wonders of Private Subscription Memberships.

## Private Subscription Memberships

Let's just suppose for a moment that you have some piece of knowledge you can deliver to your audience that doesn't involve you personally 'teaching' them a thought-out programme.

Perhaps you keep up to date with employment law and are in a position to offer regular updates on the changes to corporate clients. Maybe you have a huge collection of delicious recipes that will keep you slim and you can suggest well-balanced weekly menus. Or you are great at children's craft ideas and can come up with regular projects for busy mums to entertain their kids.

The basics are simple: you ask people to pay you a monthly subscription fee and in return you send them regular information or even a physical product. What you can charge once again depends on your level of expertise or the monetary value to your client of the information you are going to provide. A membership could be charged out at anything from £5 a month to £500 a month depending on your know- how and the subject matter.

A membership can also be a paid alternative to a community-based Facebook Group: for example, for my skincare business consultancy I run a free business group where I encourage people to give each other support and information. I spend very little time on there myself but because it is free it helps me to build my audience. I also run a private (paid) subscriber membership Facebook Group for those who want direct access to me.

In the subscriber membership, participants get a live group Q&A once a month, the opportunity to book a one-to-one 20-minute 'hot seat coaching session' with me. I do just two a month and they are streamed to the group so everyone can benefit from the information. I also invite experts to come in once a month and give presentations on topics I feel my group will benefit from. I do not pay the experts; instead, they get the opportunity to promote their own programmes during the session. This works really well. I currently charge £35 a month (six months' minimum) to subscribe to this Group and with very little promotion I currently have 80 members. Many of the members are clients who have previously bought my consultancy packages so for me the private membership is also a way to keep in touch once their private coaching with me has ended.

Let's think of other ways you could use this option:

Maybe you are an expat sunning yourself in Spain or France or Italy or wherever.

There are some very successful memberships that offer conversational language groups where newcomers can come once a week to meet new people and practice talking in a foreign tongue. You don't need to be a language teacher to do this, you just have to offer a weekly topic and you could circulate a list of key words that members could use in the next session. Most importantly, you can have fun with this and get paid at the same time. If you have lived in the new country for a long time another option is to offer administrative help or advice to help newcomers to settle in.

Maybe you are great at DIY. How about doing a series of one-minute problem-solving videos on the most common issues people have: how to change the cistern in a bathroom, bleed a radiator, how to put up a shelf etc. Thinks... You could call yourself 'Mr. Mend It'. This concept could be replicated across a hundred skills. What people tend to forget when they find something easy to do is that there are millions out there who, given the same challenge, wouldn't know where to start.

If you already have a Facebook Group that you set up for social purposes, you might also want to think about how you could monetize that. Your group may have been set up to entertain people of a certain demographic with specific shared interests and if you have built the group with passion the chances are your audience already trusts and loves you. Perhaps, they would love to buy T-shirts or tote bags that show they belong to your group or perhaps you could offer a second, paid tier where they can access workshops on topics you think might interest them. Here of course I am talking about generating income for you but if you are uncomfortable with that you could offer to give a percentage of the revenue to a charity.

The great thing about memberships is that they generate community, which I guarantee you will enjoy, and when you have a strong community, people within it generate their own content for the group. Memberships also work brilliantly when your content is predictable, so people know what is happening on a certain day of the week. This means you can sit down for a few hours every couple of months, put your content together and then use a scheduling tool like www.hootsuite.com, www.buffer.com, or even Facebook's own advance scheduling tool. All these apps will publish your content for you automatically on dates that you specify in advance. This is really the best way to work because if you feel you have to look for new ideas and new content all the time your enthusiasm will turn to stress and, interestingly, one of the most common reasons people drop out of membership sites is because they feel overwhelmed by too much information. Keep it colourful, entertaining and predictable and stick to one key theme each month and you will retain a loyal following.

Here is an example: let's say you have a membership about growing wonderful vegetables. Your monthly membership programme could look something like this:

Mondays: 'What to do in your garden this week

Wednesdays: 'Spotlight on' Sprouts, or Pumpkins or Potatoes or whatever ... maybe their history, varieties, soil requirements, folklore etc.)

Fridays: Gardeners' Question Time – a Facebook Live or Zoom (maybe once a month)

You could also do a 'Show & Tell' to get your community involved, perhaps a video tour of your own plot, something on pests or harvesting or storage – the point is there are enough different vegetables to allow you to stretch consistent content over several years using the same topics headings. You could also invite experts in to talk about their prize tomatoes or you could run your own competitions within the membership: 'Who grew the largest marrow?'

## Email marketing

If you have some hard information you can share maybe weekly, such as horse-racing or stock market tips then the membership subscription model would also work perfectly for you, bringing in regular income, and all you have to do is to deliver it in a weekly or monthly email to your membership subscribers. No need for a group, a programme or anything else at all – being successful at this is just about building your email list through self-promotion on social media, setting up a landing page where people can subscribe and maybe building relationships with Affiliate Partners so you can reach as many people as possible.

## YouTube

YouTube is a very interesting phenomenon in the social media arena, as it is primarily a search engine that people use when they want to find information. It's actually owned by Google.

Most of the social media platforms want you to pay them to advertise on their platforms rather than just share information for free and their algorithms are set up so that adverts are seen by far more people than your unpaid posts are. So with Facebook and Instagram etc. quality comes before quantity, as they will only promote free posts if they feel they are particularly engaging.

YouTube on the other hand values quantity above quality. In fact when you have created a list of 1000 subscribers and have attracted 4000 watch hours, YouTube makes you a partner and they start paying you to post videos!

In order for your videos to attract a large audience you need to create an excellent Title slide, thumbnail and descriptive text that includes a lot of keyword tags so people looking for what you are offering can find you easily.

You can create YouTube videos on your phone (use landscape format) or, if you have a Mac you could use the free Photo Booth App that comes with it. Mac also gives you iMovie for free and that is an excellent editing tool. Also check out Camtasia for creating video tutorials and presentations or, simpler still, go on to https://fiverr.com and pay someone to edit for you.

Eight minutes is the ideal length for a YouTube video and that should give you enough time to put an advert in the middle of your clip should you want to. The important thing is to keep your information to the point and to get to that point fast.

YouTube has a lot of tools that will give you data on your audience, the length of time they stay watching and whether or not they share the clip. Building your audience is, to a large degree, a matter of trial and error so you need to regularly check and learn from what the data is telling you.

Hopefully, by now one of the above option outlines has helped you choose how you are going to deliver your programme. All that is really left for you to learn now is how to find and retain your clients.

# "Build it and they will come"

No, they frigging won't! They will only come if you consistently let your audience know you are there to genuinely help/inform/entertain them. You also need to make them love you, so you have to get out there, make yourself visible and build some trust before you try to sell anything. The more information you give away for free (ouch, that hurts), the more likely people are to invest in further learning from you.

When you start exploring the world of internet programme launches you will undoubtedly come across a number of coaches trying to sell you 'tried and tested formulas' for launching your product. The broad idea is to reel people in, i.e. you start by giving them valuable tidbits on your Instagram page or in your Facebook Group, then you set up a free Webinar on a topic they cannot resist and during that Webinar you offer them a time-sensitive, bonus-loaded deal if they sign up to your paid programme. After that you bombard the ones who haven't signed up with some juicy emails and you also set a closing date for registration to your programme so that with every email they receive people become more and more conscious that time is running out and if they don't act now they are going to miss out on some phenomenal, supersonic, not-to-be-missed piece of greatness!

You will also see marketing experts talking about 'funnels' which, in addition to the above process, can involve getting people to sign up to a very cheap product and once they have bought it and got to know you better 'upselling' them increasingly more expensive packages until they finally reach your top of the range, 45k a day, 18-carat gold, luxury Ding dong package.

Now the thing is that, love it or hate it, funnels do tend to work but if like me the idea of them leaves you cowering in the corner in foetal position remind yourself that even though great marketing is a science that no entrepreneur should ignore, authenticity is your number one asset so beware of sacrificing authenticity in your effort to follow a formula.

If you want to look at launch techniques, I can recommend you read the afore-mentioned Jeff Walker's book *Launch*.

Since you have stayed with me this long, I feel like we are friends and I really don't want to lose you on the final run so I'm going to predict and explain a number of feelings/questions you might find yourself struggling with when you go out there into the product launch world.

» **You hate the thought of being 'pushy and sales-y and sending out endless emails'**
Any advertising agency will tell you that a consumer needs to see an advert at least seven times before they take action on it. There is even a name for it: 'the rule of 7'.

» **If I keep pestering people with emails, they will unsubscribe from my mailing list.**
Yes, they will but you shouldn't take that personally. People who unsubscribe from your list are those who would never have bought your programmes anyway. It is the ones who stay with you that you should be focusing on. That is why one of your main aims in the early stages of your business should be

to drive people to sign up to your mailing list and continuously make efforts to add to it.

» **If I do a two-hour free Webinar, then people will get to see my true value.**
Nope, they will probably leave halfway through. The ideal length for a Webinar is between 30 and 60 minutes with 15 minutes for questions at the end. It is good to have your sales pitch somewhere in the middle rather than at the end. And surprisingly, while you may think that the best time to run a Webinar is at the end of the day when people are relaxing, actually the best time has proved to be 11a.m. on a Tuesday morning.

» **If I keep my programme/membership cheap then people will be more likely to buy it.**
Pile it high and sell it cheap really doesn't work in this market. People will buy products if they are inspiring, special and interesting and, no matter what the price, the most important factor is to get people to see the value in your offer. (Would you really settle for egg and onion when what you are really hankering after is the chopped liver?)

Whether you come up with your own launch formula or follow someone else's there are a couple of golden rules that will help you to attract new potential customers.

The first is to be consistent with your social media posts or email communications. You have to show up and show up on a regular basis or you'll simply get lost in the noise out there.

The second is to offer value. I'll repeat again that you need to give away plenty of free information before you start selling so that people learn to trust you.

Understand that social media is like being at a party. It's important when you meet new people that the conversation is two-way and not just all about you. Comment on other people's posts, seek out, support and collaborate with the influencers in your field and get to know individuals before you try and sell them something.

Be the first to offer help and advice and then when you need it people will be happy to reciprocate. Experts operating in the same space as you make much better friends than they do competitors so look to collaborate rather than to compete.

# Chapter 10

# So where are we now?

My goodness, are you still here?

Well, if you are, I would like to think that you have discovered your particular brand of wisdom, decided on the best way to deliver it, set up your website, social media pages and groups and are all set to be out there earning money. But I suspect that I haven't accomplished that for you yet.

Actually, if I have just got you seriously thinking about the possibilities and believing in yourself enough to understand that this is a genuine opportunity for you then I feel happy with the job that I have done.

Going out on your own and asking the world to buy your wisdom can be pretty scary and it might be that you feel you are going to need a bit of hand-holding along the way. I certainly did when I started.

So here it is, my own group programme, designed especially for those who are convinced they want to give this a go but want to be coached through the process. I've called it the 'Wisdom Launchpad'

You can read all about the Programme here: www.melindacoss.com/wisdom

Basically, it's a 12-week programme made up of six modules, which will dig deep into:

» Identifying your wisdom
» Finding your best route to market

» Creating your product
» Building your website
» Finding your clients
» Promotion and visibility

By the time you have completed it you'll be all kitted up with a brand new business and out there rocking it.

The programme consists of a series of six pre-recorded videos, extensive workbooks and six live one-hour Q&A sessions with me, plus a bunch of expert workshops, which will be delivered by the social media colleagues who helped me on my journey over the years.

If you buy the programme you will also become a founder member of an exclusive Facebook Group, 'The Wisdom Club', made up of all the clever people who have been brave enough to do this and – you never know – if you are single perhaps we could arrange a *shidduch* for you on there (whether personal or professional)! At the very least, when we're not working we can have some fun, listen to some Beatles music, play Kalooki, have a smoke. Oooh, I can't wait.

I do hope you believe in yourselves and in me enough to join me on this journey but otherwise, lots of love and luck to you and if you plan to give this a go, do email me at melindacoss@gmail.com and let me know how you are getting on. I'm going to miss you.

For more information go to :
https:// www.melindacoss.com/wisdom

The End